Woodland and Forest

Written by Jamie Ambrose

Additional text: David Burnie and Linda Gamlin

Penguin Random House

Senior editor Gill Pitts
Editors Radhika Haswani, Olivia Stanford
Editorial assistance Cécile Landau
Senior art editor Ann Cannings
Art editor Kanika Kalra
Illustrators Abby Cook, Dan Crisp, Molly Lattin
Cartography co-ordinator Rajesh Mishra
Jacket co-ordinator Francesca Young
Jacket designers Dheeraj Arora, Amy Keast, Faith Nelson
DTP designers Syed Md. Farhan, Dheeraj Singh

Picture researcher Deepak Negi
Producer, pre-production Nadine King
Producer Isabell Schart
Managing editor Laura Gilbert
Deputy managing editor Vineetha Mokkil
Managing art editors Neha Ahuja Chowdhry, Diane Peyton Jones
Art director Martin Wilson
Publisher Sarah Larter
Publishing director Sophie Mitchell

First published in Great Britain in 2017 by
Dorling Kindersley Limited
80 Strand, London, WC2R 0RL

Copyright © 2017 Dorling Kindersley Limited
A Penguin Random House Company
10 9 8 7 6 5 4 3 2 1
001–298586 –Mar/2017

A CIP catalogue record for this book is available from the British Library.
ISBN: 978-0-2412-8252-6

Printed and bound in China.

The publisher would like to thank the following for their kind permission to reproduce their photographs:
(Key: a-above; b-below/bottom; c-centre; f-far; l-left; r-right; t-top)
4 123RF.com: Michael Truchon (cr). Dorling Kindersley: Barnabas Kindersley (bl). 5 Alamy Stock Photo: WILDLIFE GmbH (c). 7 iStockphoto.com: Henk Bentlage (br). 8–9 iStockphoto.com: IngaNielsen (Background). 8 iStockphoto.com: Imgorthand (clb). 10 Fotolia: Eric Isselee (cl). 12 123RF.com: Filipe Frazao (cb). 13 Alamy Stock Photo: Dinodia Photos (crb). iStockphoto.com: Guenter Guni (bl). 14 123RF.com: dink101 (cl). 14–15 iStockphoto.com: Oleksandr Smushko (b). 17 123RF.com: Tamara Kulikova (cl). iStockphoto.com: PinkForest (crb). 18 Dorling Kindersley: British Wildlife Centre, Surrey, UK (crb). 19 Getty Images: Frank Pali (b). 20 Corbis: Dieter Heinemann / Westend61 (tr). 21 Corbis: Don Johnston / All Canada Photos (ca). Dreamstime.com: Mykola Ivashchenko (bl). 22 Alamy Stock Photo: WILDLIFE GmbH (bc); Jixue Yang (tr). 23 Alamy Stock Photo: Helene Rogers / Art Directors & TRIP (cb); Paul R. Sterry / Nature Photographers Ltd (ca). Corbis: Martin R,gner / Westend61 (cr). 24 iStockphoto.com: jax10289 (bl). 24–25 123RF.com: Sonya Etchison (cb). 25 123RF.com: Michael Truchon (ca). 26 Fotolia: Eric Isselee (crb). 27 Dorling Kindersley: British Wildlife Centre, Surrey, UK (cr). iStockphoto.com: Ivan Strba (r). 28 iStockphoto.com: Atelopus (l); Guenter Guni (cr). 30 iStockphoto.com: IMNATURE (c); mazzzur (br); servickuz (cl). 31 Alamy Stock Photo: Klaus Ulrich Müller (cr). SuperStock: Josef Beck / imageBROKER (br). 32 iStockphoto.com: Alatom (bl). 32–33 iStockphoto.com: robas (c). 33 iStockphoto.com: davidevison (crb). 35 Dorling Kindersley: Barnabas Kindersley (c). Dreamstime.com: Alexander Pladdet (clb); Rudmer Zwerver (cb). iStockphoto.com: Saso Novoselic (br). 38 iStockphoto.com: AustralianCamera (crb). 39 Getty Images: Kathy Collins (l). 40 Alamy Stock Photo: Buiten-Beeld / Hillebrand Breuker (cr). iStockphoto.com: Thomas Faull (clb). 41 iStockphoto.com: Dennis Donohue (bl); GlobalP (cra). 45 123RF.com: hxdyl (tl). 46 iStockphoto.com: 4kodiak (cb). 47 Alamy Stock Photo: Pulsar Images (crb). 48 iStockphoto.com: Henk Bentlage (cr). 49 Alamy Stock Photo: Kenneth Walters (tl). iStockphoto.com: USO (br). 50 Dreamstime.com: Mrrgraz (clb). iStockphoto.com: Henrik_L (cr); Paulina Lenting-Smulder (l). 52 iStockphoto.com: Roger Rosentreter (cl). 52–53 iStockphoto.com: Aleksandr_Gromov (bl). 53 123RF.com: anticiclo (cla). 54 Alamy Stock Photo: Premaphotos (crb). iStockphoto.com: Jeff Goulden (cl).55 123RF.com: Diogo Baptista (cl). Alamy Stock Photo: Design Pics Inc / Michael DeYoung (tl). 58 Alamy Stock Photo: Edward Krupa (cra). iStockphoto.com: YinYang (clb). 59 iStockphoto.com: Pierre-Yves Babelon (ca)

Cover images: Front: Dreamstime.com: Liligraphie bc; Back: iStockphoto.com: Ninell_Art tl

All other images © Dorling Kindersley
For further information see: www.dkimages.com

Deciduous tree leaves are green in summer.

Spruce needles have square sides.

The wake-robin is also called trillium.

Poison dart frogs live in the rainforest.

Jay feather

Acorns are a favourite food for squirrels.

Contents

Looking at forests

Trees may grow beside your home, or in a nearby park or square. However, while it's easy to look at a single tree, exploring a forest, where trees surround you, is different. These natural "living cities" will reveal their secrets – and inhabitants – more easily if you follow a few simple rules.

Make sure you dress for the outdoors. Wear warm, waterproof clothes if it is cold or wet.

No talking on the trail

For the best chance of seeing animals, keep as quiet as you can. Wild creatures don't like noise. Remember to stay on obvious paths or trails so you don't damage their habitat, or lose your way!

WHAT KIND OF TREE?

Trees come in all shapes and sizes. No two look exactly alike, but every tree's shape can help you identify what species it is. Here are some examples of common tree shapes.

CONICAL
Alder

GNARLED
Sessile oak

SPREADING
Hornbeam

BROAD
Beech

NARROW
Silver birch

COLUMNAR
Italian cypress

What is a forest?

A forest is a large area of land, so thickly covered by trees that little light reaches the ground. Different types of forest grow in different parts of the world. Forests provide food and shelter for many different animals.

Conifers such as the Norway spruce have green, needle-like leaves.

Look up!
More animals live in forests than anywhere else on Earth. Many of them keep to the tops of trees. How many animals can you spot up there?

Coniferous forests

Coniferous forests contain tall, slender trees, such as pines or spruces, that make cones to produce seeds. They keep their needle-shaped leaves throughout the year.

Pine cones

This beech leaf is a typical wide and flat deciduous leaf.

Rainforest leaves come in all shapes and sizes.

Deciduous forests

The broader, spreading trees of deciduous forests have flat, green leaves in spring and summer that fall off in autumn. Trees such as beeches and oaks grow here.

Sweet chestnuts

Rainforests

Rainforests get lots of rain all year round. Some are so packed with different types of tree that raindrops take 10 minutes to reach the ground!

Red ginger flower

Where are forests found?

Forests cover about a third of the Earth's surface. As long as they get enough water, and temperatures are not too hot or too cold, they can grow almost anywhere. However, no matter where they are found, no two forests will look exactly the same.

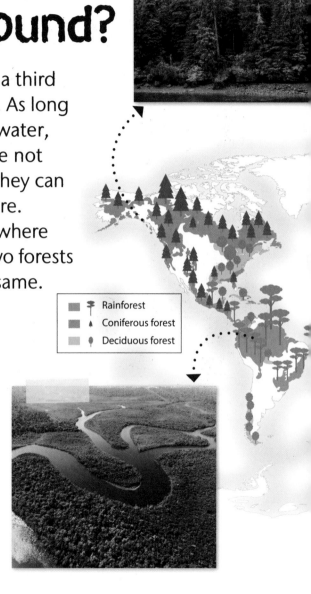

- 🌴 Rainforest
- 🌲 Coniferous forest
- 🌳 Deciduous forest

Amazon Rainforest, South America

This is the largest tropical rainforest on Earth, and more than half of it is found in Brazil. The Amazon Rainforest is so big that a fifth of all the world's bird species live here!

Tongass National Forest, Alaska

The largest national forest in the United States, Tongass is made up of spruce, hemlock, and cedar trees.

Black Forest, Germany

Germany's mountainous forest is called the "Black Forest" because the spruce trees grow so close together that parts of it are very dark to walk through!

Sundarbans, Asia

Mostly in Bangladesh, the Sundarbans is a mangrove forest. Mangrove trees grow well in wet, salty conditions, such as saltwater swamps.

Congo Rainforest, Africa

This rainforest is home to rare animals, such as lowland gorillas and forest elephants. Some parts are so dense, no one has ever seen them.

13

Coniferous forests

Most conifers are tough trees that can cope with extreme weather conditions. Their hard, needle-like leaves do not dry out as easily as the wide leaves of broad-leaved trees, so they do well in hot, dry climates, such as around the Mediterranean. They can also withstand cold, icy winters – the largest coniferous forests are in Russia and Canada.

Needle leaves

Many conifers, such as pine trees, have leaves that are shaped like needles. However, some conifers have leaves that are strap-like or scale-like. Almost all are thick, tough, and resinous.

Conifers grow tall and straight.

Sausage trees

Cones got their name because some, such as pine cones, are conical in shape. However, spruce cones are more like sausages, hanging down from the tree. Their needles also point downwards, helping them to shed snow.

Spruce needles have square sides.

Monkey puzzle

The monkey puzzle is an umbrella-shaped tree with sharply pointed leaves, which are arranged in a spiral. Also called the Chile pine, these trees are found in Chile and Argentina.

The leaf tips of monkey puzzle trees have sharp spines.

Conifers have flexible branches so that heavy snow and ice can slide off, which stops them from breaking.

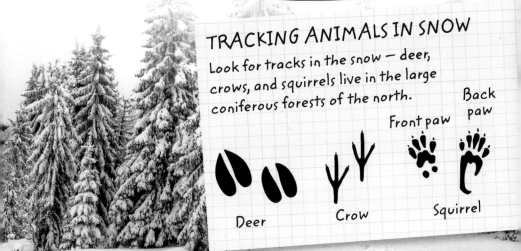

TRACKING ANIMALS IN SNOW

Look for tracks in the snow — deer, crows, and squirrels live in the large coniferous forests of the north.

Deer

Crow

Front paw

Back paw

Squirrel

Coniferous plants

Since conifers stay green all year, little sunlight reaches the forest floor. Also, conifer needles are acidic, like the juice of a lemon. When they break down they make the soil acidic too. The lack of light and acidic soil mean fewer plants grow here than elsewhere, but there are still many to spot.

Berry bearers

Scrambling plants, such as the blackberry, thrive in conifer forests. Their thorny vines allow them to climb up and over other plants towards the light, and the berries they produce provide food for animals and birds.

Blackberries make a tasty snack for foxes and deer.

Ferns

Ferns are flowerless plants, many of which love moist, shady conditions. This deer fern won't grow taller than 50 cm (20 in), but the giant chain fern, which grows underneath redwood trees, can be nearly 2 m (6.5 ft) tall!

Forest flowers provide nectar for passing insects.

Shrubs

You'll see few flowers in a coniferous forest, but some shrubs, such as wild roses, can bloom beneath the needles. They are found in the north of the United States, northern Europe, and Asia.

Lichens

Open conifer forests are home to lichens. These sponge-like growths are not plants, but are a partnership between an alga and a fungus. Reindeer lichen is a vital food for caribou in winter and can cover an entire forest floor.

Mosses

Mosses are simple plants known as bryophytes. They can't move water around their bodies, but instead soak it up like sponges. Like ferns, mosses produce no flowers. They release tiny spores to reproduce.

Coniferous forest animals

Many animals make their home in coniferous forests, especially in winter, when the trees provide shelter from snow. Some animals would not be able to live anywhere else, because they only eat things that live and grow in a coniferous forest.

Scots pine cones

Red squirrel

The crossbill uses its unique beak to tease out seeds from cones.

Cone specialists

Seeds from pine and other conifer cones are the main food for many birds, such as the crossbill, and small mammals. Some, such as squirrels, hide cones in secret larders to make sure they have enough food in winter.

Moose

The moose is the forest's largest grazing animal. In summer, it eats grass and other plants, but in winter it eats pine and spruce needles. Not many animals can do this!

Top predators

Meat-eaters like grey wolves hunt other animals that live in the forest. When hunting alone, they catch small mammals like hares or mice, but as a pack they can bring down a moose or deer.

Deciduous forests

In a deciduous forest, all or most of the trees lose their leaves when summer ends. Apart from a few evergreens, the trees shut down for the winter. When spring arrives, the Sun beams through to the forest floor until the trees have grown their new leaves. So in spring, flowers cover these forest floors like a carpet.

Sweet chestnut leaves

Long leaves

Sweet chestnut trees are easy to recognize. Their leaves are the longest in the forest and their bark often spirals round the trunk.

Winter leaves

Beech leaves are very smooth and shiny on top, with a wavy edge. Young beeches may keep their foliage in the winter, even though the leaves are dead and brown.

Beech leaves

Jagged edges

The basic shape of most oak leaves is the same, but their edges can be different. White oak leaves are jagged. In autumn, look for acorns that have fallen from the trees.

White oak leaves

Unlike deciduous trees, the leaves of coniferous trees stay green all year.

The leaves of deciduous trees may turn red, orange, or yellow.

Blazing forest

Some forests become a blaze of red and yellow just before the leaves fall. The most colourful displays are in the United States and Canada, because of the trees that grow there.

Look for worms, beetles, and many other animals living in the leaf litter.

Lovely litter

When leaves fall, they build up into leaf litter on the forest floor. Unlike man-made litter such as crisp packets, this litter will decompose (break down).

Dormice like to hide among dead leaves.

21

Broad-leaved

The leaves of broad-leaved trees come in many different shapes and sizes. They are called broad because they are thin, flat, and often wide. In North America and Europe, most broad-leaved trees are deciduous. In most other parts of the world, they are evergreen.

Lots of leaves
At the end of summer, many broad-leaved trees drop their leaves. Enough leaves may fall from one tree to make a heap 2 m (6.5 ft) high, which would cover you!

Broader leaves
Norway maples have leaves that are sometimes broader than they are long. Most maples have hand-shaped leaves. Stretch your fingers as wide as you can to see the basic shape.

Veins carry food and water around the leaf.

The pattern of the veins can help you identify a tree.

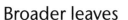

Stripy snake

Not all maple leaves are hand-shaped. This snakebark maple leaf is shaped like an arrowhead. Snakebark maples have stripy bark, so can you guess how they got their name?

This snakebark leaf has jagged edges and a pointed tip.

Leaves within leaves

Some leaves look as if they have been cut into smaller leaves with a pair of scissors. Ash trees have leaves like this. They are called compound leaves.

RUB A LEAF

You can make a record of vein patterns by laying a leaf from a broad-leaved tree upside down and putting paper over it. Rub the paper gently with a soft pencil and see the pattern appear. Remember to label your leaf rubbing when you have finished.

23

Woodland flowers

All plants need light to grow. However, woods are often quite dark. So how do woodland flowers manage to survive? In woods where the trees shed their leaves every year, many plants grow and flower in spring before the trees have grown new leaves.

Trees in bloom

Many trees, particularly those growing on the edge of a forest, produce flowers themselves in spring. Some, like these eastern redbuds, which are native to North America, are also planted in parks and gardens.

Wood anemone

Delicate, star-shaped wood anemones are one of the first flowers to appear on the forest floor in spring, particularly in older or ancient woodlands.

Wake-robin

The wake-robin is a woodland flower that grows mainly in North America and eastern Asia. Each flower has just three petals. The Native Americans who once lived in the woods made medicines from its fat underground roots.

Green sepals protect the flower as it grows.

The wake-robin is also called trillium.

The flower has three pointed petals.

Bluebells

Dazzling bluebells create a purple-blue haze in British woodlands in springtime. They are an important source of food for insects emerging after winter.

Food for all

Wild violets provide food for many creatures. Butterflies and tiny ants feed on their nectar, but other insects eat their leaves. Even deer and rabbits nibble their foliage, while mice and birds feast on their seeds.

25

Deciduous forest animals

A wide variety of creatures of all sizes live in deciduous forests. These range from tiny insects to huge grazing animals, such as deer, or even large black bears in North America. However, they all have to be able to adapt to the changing seasons in order to survive.

Birds

Birds of all types live in broadleaf forests. Most are easier to hear than to see, especially in spring, when they fill the forest with songs. Some, such as the tawny owl, sleep during the day, so they're almost impossible to spot.

Tawny owls hunt small mammals at night.

Squirrels

Grey squirrel

Red squirrel

Unlike many mammals, squirrels don't sleep through the winter so they need to collect and store food for the colder months. Nuts keep well and squirrels collect them in autumn.

Foxes

Foxes are common forest residents on many continents. These crafty predators hunt small mammals, such as rabbits, for food. They also eat berries, insects, reptiles, eggs, and food dropped or left by humans. They're not fussy!

Foxes have broad, bushy tails called brushes.

Deer

Deer are among the largest forest inhabitants. They eat new leaves and tree bark as well as grasses, shoots, and leaves. Woodlands provide shelter from the weather and hide them from predators, including human hunters.

Red deer are the largest land animals in the UK.

Creepy-crawlies

Earthworms, beetles, and woodlice eat leaves and rotting bark, turning them into rich soil. Spiders and centipedes hunt the leaf-eaters, while slugs and snails feed on all kinds of debris and forest fungi.

How many bugs can you spot on the forest floor?

Rainforests

Unlimited moisture and plenty of sunlight mean that trees can grow and grow – and that's exactly what happens in a tropical rainforest. The trees compete frantically with each other for the light, and reach tremendous heights as a result.

Teeming with life

Scientists think that over half of all the plant and animal species in the world, some not yet discovered, live in rainforest habitats. Many are found nowhere else on Earth.

Vital forests

Rainforests produce 20 per cent of the oxygen we need to breathe. They also absorb the greenhouse gas carbon dioxide, which helps control climate change and keeps the planet's weather stable.

Living layers

A tropical rainforest is like a tall building that has several different floors. Scientists call these "strata" or layers.

Emergents

Only the tallest trees, called "emergents", stick out of the highest layer.

Canopy

Usually between 20–40 m (65–130 ft) above ground, the canopy is hot and fairly dry. Most animals live here.

Understory

Shaded by the canopy, but still well above ground, this is the realm of ferns, vines, and smaller animals.

Shrub layer

As this layer is very dark, shorter plants and young trees compete to get the most sunlight.

Forest floor

The hottest, darkest, and dampest layer, the forest floor is covered with dead leaves and is alive with insects.

Rainforest plants

In tropical rainforests, where it is always wet and very warm, plants grow and flower all year round. Many different plants grow here, and some are very unusual, but all are specially adapted to their surroundings and could not grow in the wild anywhere else.

The vanilla orchid has yellow flowers.

Orchids can be grown as houseplants.

Amazing orchids

At least 10,000 different orchids grow in rainforests. Most get the water they need from moisture in the air, so they don't need soil to grow in. One of these, the vanilla orchid, is the source of the vanilla pods used to flavour ice cream!

Rafflesia smells so awful that it is also called the "corpse flower".

Giant parasite

Rafflesia has the largest single flower on Earth, growing to over 1 m (3 ft) across and weighing 11 kg (24 lb). This southeast Asian plant lives most of its life inside a vine, stealing food from a "host" plant, until it blooms.

Passionflower nectar is a favourite food for hummingbirds.

Hanging around

As vines, passionflowers climb up other plants and hang on by their curly tendrils. Bees and hummingbirds visit their flowers, but they must be quick because each blossom lasts for just a single day.

Poison dart frogs can be found in bromeliad "ponds".

Useful bromeliads

You already know one bromeliad – the pineapple – but these rainforest plants come in many varieties. They can grow on the ground, on rocks, or even on other plants. Their overlapping leaves hold rainwater, which provides a "pond" for insects and frogs high up in the trees.

Super lily

Each season, a giant water lily produces 40 to 50 leaves, but this is not why it is so special. A leaf of this South American rainforest plant can grow to more than 2.5 m (8 ft) across.

Rainforest animals

From mammals and birds to amphibians and insects, more animals live in rainforests than in any other habitat. Some of the largest are peaceful plant eaters, while the smallest may pack a deadly punch. Many of these animals blend in so well with their environment that they cannot be spotted easily.

Hidden hunter

The jaguar is one of the Amazon Rainforest's most secretive animals. It hunts at dusk or dawn, when its spotted coat provides the perfect camouflage. It even hunts in water, sometimes catching prey much bigger than itself.

Gardener of the forest

Wild orangutans are found on just two islands, Borneo and Sumatra, in Asia. Although highly endangered because of habitat loss, as fruit eaters, they help new trees to grow by spreading seeds around.

Orangutans are excellent climbers.

Out of the blue

With warm conditions and plenty of flowers, rainforests make ideal homes for butterflies. The metallic-looking blue morpho butterfly has a 13–20 cm (5–8 in) wingspan. It lives mainly in the canopy of Central and South American rainforests.

Treetop dweller

One of the strangest-looking Asian rainforest birds, the rhinoceros hornbill spends most of its time in treetops. Its horn-shaped beak acts like an amplifier, making its calls extra loud.

Small but deadly

The poison dart frog's bright colours warn predators to stay away. Some species of this Central and South American resident are so toxic that just licking its skin could be fatal to hungry hunters!

Forest detective

The next time you are out in a forest, see how many different things you can find. Start by looking carefully at your surroundings – binoculars and a magnifying glass can help here. Why not take a notebook and pencil along to write down any important observations?

Tree gall

Galls are grape-like growths on leaves, branches, or bark. Those made by insects, such as wasps, have a developing grub inside.

Open brown cones mean fine weather.

Closed green cones are not ripe yet!

Pine cones

Cones are nature's weather predictors. Open ones mean the air is dry and the weather should stay fine. Closed ones mean the air is moist and it might rain.

Owl pellet

A clump of fur and bones beneath a tree shows that an owl has roosted nearby. Soak the pellet in water and gently tease it apart with tweezers to find out what the owl has eaten.

These tiny mammal bones belong to a vole or mouse.

Jay feather

Discarded feathers tell you which birds are found in a forest. A bright-blue feather like this belongs to a jay. See what others you can find and identify.

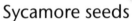

Sycamore seeds

Winged seeds or "keys" on a woodland floor mean sycamores, ash, or maple trees are growing nearby. Try to match the seed to the tree.

Voles open nuts with their sharp teeth.

Hazelnuts

Where there are nuts, there are nut eaters. Look closely at holes in hazelnut or acorn shells to find teeth marks left by hungry voles, squirrels, or mice.

How a forest forms

A forest does not appear overnight. It takes years, sometimes centuries, before tiny seedlings grow into tall, majestic trees. Just like humans, a forest starts small, then grows and develops through many different stages. This is called "succession".

Events such as fires, storms, flooding, and logging can severely delay forest succession.

Shrubland

After several years, taller, thicker-stemmed shrubs start to grow. They crowd out the grasses and other plants. Some of these shrubs include small trees, which eventually grow taller than the rest of the plants.

Herbs, grasses, and ferns

Bare ground is just what short, grassy plants like to grow in. Once grasses start to grow, tougher and taller plants such as herbs move in, and so do some ferns, such as bracken.

Bare ground

Everything starts with a firm base – in a forest's case, this means a patch of bare ground.

Mature forest

After 50 to 150 years or so, what was once a young forest is now filled with bigger, sturdier trees. The canopy is thicker and fewer shrubs grow beneath it, unless some trees die or lose branches, letting in more light.

Young forest

After about 25 to 50 years, younger, faster-growing trees have taken over the site, shading out many of the smaller shrubs. The leaves they shed each year also change the nutrients in the soil.

Changing seasons

In some parts of the world, there is a huge difference between the seasons – between summer and winter, or between the dry season and the rainy season. Trees have to adapt to the changing seasons as best they can. Some lose all their leaves in the winter or the dry season, while others shed just some of their leaves.

Small change

Forests near the equator – such as this rainforest in northeastern Australia – have just about the same climate all year round. The further you travel from the equator, the more the temperature changes between seasons.

KEEP A RECORD

Take a photo of your favourite tree at different times of the year, so you can see how its leaves grow and change.

Spring

In spring, deciduous trees produce new leaves. The leaves start their lives curled up inside buds, which expand quickly. The trees can then begin making food.

Summer

During summer, the leaves grow darker and tougher to keep hungry leaf-eating insects at bay. Some trees grow another set of leaves to replace those that have been eaten.

Autumn

A substance called chlorophyll makes leaves green. Before their leaves fall, trees break down their chlorophyll and the leaves may become red or yellow before finally turning brown.

Winter

The trees become dormant, which means they rest until spring, so their leaves are not needed to make food. During winter the branches are bare. New leaves will grow in spring and the cycle starts again.

Looking up

While some animals live among the roots and trunks of trees, many others go about their daily business high up in the branches. The next time you walk through a forest, don't forget to look up. There is a lot of life happening overhead!

Who lives where?

Many birds and mammals nest in holes in trees. In parts of Europe, you might see young, ferret-like pine martens peeking out of their cosy den. In spring you may spy a bird carrying nest materials, such as twigs or moss.

Hunt for hitchhikers

Mistletoe is a parasite that attaches itself to trees and takes nutrients from them. Its roots grow right into the wood of the host tree.

Mistletoe forms recognizable balls high up in tree branches.

What's moving?

The best way to observe a forest canopy is to lie down and look up. You might see squirrels high up in the trees, or even raccoons in a North American forest. In the rainforest, you may be lucky enough to spot a bright-red macaw.

Autumn harvest

In autumn, animals gather food to store for the winter. Some birds, such as the acorn woodpecker, drill holes in tree trunks to store acorns. Fewer leaves mean animals are easier to see, so look up to enjoy more than just the changing leaf colours.

NAME THAT BIRD

See how many different birds you can spot in the canopy. The best time to hear and see them is at dawn in spring, when males sing to attract females.

Life in a log

A fallen log might look dead, but in fact it is teeming with life. Home to all sorts of different tiny animals, plants, lichens, and fungi, logs also provide a safe place for seedlings to grow. This is why they are sometimes called "nurse logs".

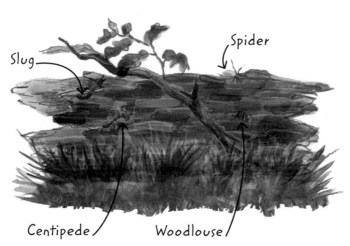

Slug

Spider

Centipede

Woodlouse

Newly fallen
Once a log falls, slugs and woodlice are among the first creatures to find shelter in the dark, moist places beneath it. They feed on decaying plants, and centipedes and spiders follow to eat them!

One year old
After one year, new creatures have moved in. Bark bugs live beneath the bark, while beetles drill holes to lay their eggs in. Their larvae eat the rotting wood. Mosses and fungi, such as ink cap mushrooms, appear on the log's surface.

Beetle

Moss

Woodpecker

Stag beetle

Wasp

Two years old

Full of holes and with crumbling bark, after two years the log is almost completely covered in lichens, fungi, and mosses. Wasps and stag beetles nest here, and woodpeckers come to feast on their grubs and larvae.

Fungi

WHAT CAN YOU FIND?

If you find a fallen log, make a list of all the plants and animals you can see living on it. Return to the same log after some time has passed to see what changes have occurred.

Why we need forests

Besides providing homes and food for countless animals, trees supply us with a useful gift: wood. The first tools made by humans were probably sticks used for digging up roots. We still depend on wood and use it in dozens of different ways – to build houses, boats, furniture, toys, and much more!

Sap with a bounce

Rubber is the gummy sap that comes from rubber trees. It is collected by tapping – making cuts in the bark and gathering the sticky juice that flows out. This juice is then turned into rubber to make car and bicycle tyres, footballs, and rubber bands.

Crafty cork

Cork comes from the bark of the cork oak – a tree that grows around the Mediterranean. It is used for flooring, placemats, and champagne corks.

Festive favourite

In some countries, conifer trees are decorated for Christmas. These trees were originally cut down where they grew in forests. Today they are grown in specially planted Christmas-tree farms.

From pulp to paper

We make paper from wood. In factories called paper mills, tree trunks are ground up into pulp – a mushy substance that is then pressed, dried, dyed, and formed into paper products.

Paper is made in giant rolls in paper mills.

MAKING PAPER

You can recycle used paper to make new paper. To do this at home you will need newspaper, wire netting that an adult has nailed to a frame, a saucepan, and an old cloth or towel.

1. Shred clean newspaper into a saucepan of water. ASK AN ADULT to boil it until it turns into a mushy pulp.

2. When the pulp cools, pour it onto the wire netting. Let the water drain and turn the wet paper onto a clean cloth.

3. Once the pulp has become firm, hang the new paper up to dry.

You can decorate your new paper with petals or leaves.

Farming forests

Trees helped our ancestors to survive by providing them with food in the form of fruit and nuts. Much of the fruit we eat now has changed from the wild-grown food of our ancestors' day, because we grow it in artificial forests known as orchards. Some nuts and other foods, however, are still harvested from the wild.

Ancient apples

The ancestors of modern apples were tiny, sour-tasting crab apples. After thousands of years of selection by farmers, who chose trees with the largest, sweetest fruit, we now enjoy delicious apples from farmed trees.

Crab apples still grow in woodlands and hedgerows.

The world's favourite bean?

More than 2,000 years ago, people living in the rainforests of Central America discovered the fruit of the cocoa tree. Today this tree is grown around the world for its seeds, known as "beans". These are the source of all the world's chocolate!

Two from one

In Indonesia and the Caribbean, an evergreen called a nutmeg tree is grown in large plantations. Farmers harvest two spices from these trees. The seed is called nutmeg, while its lacy covering is known as mace. Both are ground up and used as spices.

Mace

Nutmeg

Wild and wonderful

Brazil-nut trees grow only in the rainforests of South America. They can be as tall as 60 m (200 ft), and are pollinated by just one species of wild rainforest bee. This means they aren't easy to grow in orchards.

Making nutshell boats

Make a nutshell boat by pressing a ball of sticky tac inside half a walnut shell. To make the sail, use a cocktail stick to pierce a leaf or piece of paper, being careful not to touch the sharp points.
Push one end of the stick into the sticky tac and it is ready to go!

Danger, keep clear!

Most forest creatures are harmless, but some bite if they feel threatened, and others, like certain caterpillars, have stinging hairs on their bodies to ward off predators. Not all plants are human-friendly, either, so unless you are sure they won't bring you out in a rash – or worse – don't touch them.

Dangerous fungi

Bright colours are often nature's warning signals, so avoid touching any yellow or red fungi. Many mushrooms and toadstools contain toxic chemicals, which, if eaten, can kill you. Some are even deadly just to touch. The safest practice is to leave all fungi alone.

Biting bugs

Many insects have bites and stings. Spider bites can be painful, and some are even deadly. Some beetles can nip if picked up and ants, bees, and wasps can sting. Ticks are stealthy, and can bite you without you feeling it. Always check yourself over after a woodland walk for stowaways.

Plants to avoid

In North American forests, simply brushing against vines, such as poison ivy and poison oak, brings many people out in an itchy rash. In any forest, look out for stinging plants such as nettles, and plants with barbs or briars, such as wild roses. Never touch or eat any berries as they can be poisonous.

Poison ivy has glossy leaves.

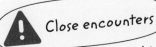

Close encounters

Most animals will avoid humans if they hear you approach, but you may be lucky enough to see some up close. If you do, stay still and give them room and time to move away. Never run from a larger animal such as a bear. It may end up chasing you!

Respect snakes

Many snakes are harmless, and most simply want to avoid humans, but you may come across one on a walk that refuses to move. Keep away and walk around it if necessary, while admiring it from a safe distance.

Forest fungi

Scientists place fungi into a separate group – or "kingdom" – of living things because fungi are neither plants nor animals. The mushroom or toadstool you see is only a tiny part of a much bigger organism that is one of nature's great recyclers.

Beneficial bracket

A shelf-like growth on a tree is called a bracket fungus. Most bracket fungi appear only on dead or dying trees. Apart from breaking down rotting wood, they also provide food for other creatures.

Dead-wood dweller

Golf ball-shaped fungi found on a rotting stump or fallen branch are most likely stump puffballs. When touched, the balls release clouds of tiny spores – each of which can become a new puffball fungus.

Deadly destroyers

Some fungi harm forests. The honey fungus attacks trees underground, killing the roots of both conifers and deciduous trees. By the time mushrooms appear on their trunk, the trees are already doomed.

Underground arrangement

Fungi create a huge underground network called a mycelium, made up of fine threads called hyphae. The fly agaric toadstool's hyphae grow around a tree's roots. The hyphae take in sugar from the roots, but add nutrients and water to the soil to feed the tree.

⚠️ Warning: Don't touch any toadstools or fungi you find — they may be poisonous.

Look for fly agaric toadstools near birch and pine trees.

The mass of threads underground is the main part of the fungus.

Forests in danger

Forests have many natural enemies, such as plants or fungi that attack them, storms that destroy whole trees, or animals that eat tree bark or leaves. People can also hurt forests by starting forest fires, cutting down too many trees, or causing harmful pollution.

Fire hazards

Some fires are helpful – many plants need the heat they cause in order for their seeds to break open and grow. But unplanned fires destroy forests, damaging plants and harming animals.

Too much cutting

Every minute, we lose a forest the size of 20 football fields. Deforestation is caused when people cut down too many trees. This happens for many reasons, such as when people want more space to plant crops, graze cattle, or build towns.

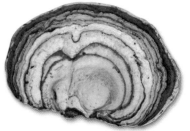

Deadly fungi
Fungi that feed on wood are among a tree's greatest enemies. The fungi push tiny feeding threads into the wood, which can infect the tree.

Rain damage
Exhaust fumes from cars, and smoke from fires, factories, and power stations all release poisonous gases into the air. When they mix with water they fall as acid rain. If the rain is too acidic, trees lose their leaves and die.

Tree stranglers
Tropical strangler figs live up to their name! They wind around a tree, smothering its trunk and branches. The tree eventually dies.

HOW YOU CAN HELP
* Reduce, reuse, and recycle. By using recycled paper products, no new forests need to be cut down.

* Eat less meat from animals that require grazing land.

* Only buy wood from companies that source wood sustainably. They don't cut down too many trees and they also plant new ones.

Friends of the forest

A forest is home to many living things. Some animals feed on trees, but others protect them by eating their enemies. This is called "mutualism" because both the animals and the trees benefit from each other. Forests also benefit humans, who in turn can help protect these natural treasures.

Best bird friends

Forests offer birds safe places to nest as well as plenty of food. In return, birds like the chickadee eat the insects that nibble on tree leaves or suck sap. Other birds eat and scatter a tree's seeds so that new trees begin to grow.

Guarding ants

Whistling thorn acacia trees have special hollow spaces at the base of their spines where ants can nest. In return for their free homes, the ferocious stinging ants keep away leaf eaters, such as antelopes.

Wide-ranging rangers

Park rangers keep forests healthy and safe, by doing everything from planting new seedlings to removing diseased trees and getting rid of pests. Some national parks have junior ranger programmes, so you can take part in many forest-related activities.

Park rangers keep an eye out for forest fires.

Fighting fire

Teams of firefighters dig trenches, clear away debris, and pump water and chemicals to put out wildfires. Firefighters often start controlled fires to keep too many leaves and twigs from building up and fuelling a larger fire. Small fires also open up space for seedlings to grow.

Forest helper
You can be a friend to your local forest or woodland by picking up litter, being careful with campfires, and reporting damaged trees.

Forest myths

All over the world, people who live near forests have told tales of many strange and often wonderful creatures thought to inhabit them. From horned horses to trolls, giant ape-like creatures to tree spirits, woodlands have long been thought of as places of magic and mystery.

Horned horse
Stories of horses with a horn on their head that lived in forests have been told since ancient times. In Europe, they are called unicorns and were said to be pure white, gentle creatures, often with magical powers.

Tree-loving trolls
In northern Europe, the forests of Scandinavia are believed by some people to be the home of forest trolls. However, no one can agree exactly on what a troll looks like.

Forest spirits

The ancient Greeks believed forests were inhabited by spirits, which they called nymphs. Nymphs were said to be beautiful girls who lived near water, mountains, or woods. Wood or tree nymphs, called dryads, were even thought to live in or near particular trees.

Wild men of the woods

Many people in North America believe that huge, hairy, ape-like creatures still live deep in the woods of the USA and Canada. This beast has been called a "bigfoot", but it is also known as a "sasquatch" or even a "wood ape".

Tricksters in the trees

In North America, Native American tribes tell stories of "little spirits" that live in forests. They are called "canoti" by some tribes and are described as being tricksters who caused hunters to lose their way.

57

Unusual forests

Most people think of forests as lots of coniferous or deciduous trees growing over a large area, or even of rainforests, which contain a wider variety of trees. The Earth is full of forests that don't fit these descriptions. Many look strange or are unusual in other ways.

Forests of stone
The remains of ancient forests still exist. Prehistoric trees were buried under mud, ice, or ash due to volcanic explosions or floods. They have turned to stone over millions of years.

Forests of grass
In Southeast Asia, you can see forests filled with tall plants, but they aren't trees. These are bamboo forests, such as the one at Anji in China. Although it can grow very tall and strong, bamboo is actually a grass.

Forest of giants

New Zealand's Waipoua Forest has the greatest number of the planet's kauri trees. These conifers are among the oldest in the world. One of the largest kauris is also the oldest, and is thought to be about 2,000 years old.

Dry-climate forests

Dry-climate forest trees have special features to help them survive. Some, such as the African baobabs, store water in their trunks and limbs – they swell during the rainy season, saving water for later use.

Swamp forests

Swamps and riversides can be tough places for trees to grow, as their roots need to breathe. Many trees, such as mangroves, arch their roots above the water's surface so that they can take in lots of air.

Index

Acknowledgements

**Dorling Kindersley
would like to thank:**

Hilary Bird for indexing.
Kathleen Teece for
editorial assistance.
Faith Nelson for
design assistance.